D.I.Y. MAKE IT HAPPEN

CRAFT FAIR

VIRGINIA LOH-HAGAN

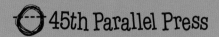
45th Parallel Press

Published in the United States of America by Cherry Lake Publishing
Ann Arbor, Michigan
www.cherrylakepublishing.com

Reading Adviser: Marla Conn MS, Ed., Literacy specialist, Read-Ability, Inc.
Book Designer: Felicia Macheske

Photo Credits: © Sergey Maksimov/Shutterstock.com, cover, 1; © Eivaisla/Shutterstock.com, cover, 1, 19; © shooarts/
Shutterstock.com, 3; © Monkey Business Images/Shutterstock.com, 5, 26; © FabrikaSimf/Shutterstock.com, 7; © Dobo
Kristian/Shutterstock.com, 9; © Africa Studio/Shutterstock.com, 10; © gezzeg/Shutterstock.com, 11; © Dmitry Zimin/
Shutterstock.com, 12, 30; © Matthew Browning/Shutterstock.com, 14; © Denis Dryashkin/Shutterstock.com, 15;
© HomeArt/Shutterstock.com, 15; © extradeda/Shutterstock.com , 17, 31; © phana sitti/Shutterstock.com, 17, 31;
© guruXOX//Shutterstock.com, 18; © Jim Jurica/iStock.com, 20; © Green Leaf/Shutterstock.com, 21, 31; © Gorosi/
Shutterstock.com, 23; © Usmanov Ramil/Shutterstock.com, 25; © Boyblackcat/Shutterstock.com, 27; © leungchopan/
Shutterstock.com, 28; © photka/Shutterstock.com, 29; © wavebreakmedia/Shutterstock.com, back cover; © Dora Zett/
Shutterstock.com, back cover

Graphic Elements Throughout: © pashabo/Shutterstock.com; © axako/Shutterstock.com; © IreneArt/Shutterstock.com;
© Katya Bogina/Shutterstock.com; © Belausava Volha/Shutterstock.com; © Nik Merkulov/Shutterstock.com; © Ya Tshey/
Shutterstock.com; © kubais/Shutterstock.com; © Sasha Nazim/Shutterstock.com; © Infomages/Shutterstock.com; © Ursa
Major/Shutterstock.com; © topform/Shutterstock.com; © Art'nLera/Shutterstock.com; © Chief Crow Daria/Shutterstock.com

45th Parallel Press is an imprint of Cherry Lake Publishing.

Library of Congress Cataloging-in-Publication Data

Names: Loh-Hagan, Virginia, author.
Title: Craft fair / by Virginia Loh-Hagan.
Description: Ann Arbor : Cherry Lake Publishing, 2017. I Series: DIY projects
  I Includes bibliographical references and index.
Identifiers: LCCN 2016029712I ISBN 9781634721431 (hardcover) I ISBN
  9781634722094 (pdf) I ISBN 9781634722759 (pbk.) I ISBN 9781634723411 (ebook)
Subjects: LCSH: Craft festivals—Planning—Juvenile literature. I
  Handicraft—Marketing—Juvenile literature.
Classification: LCC TT149 .L65 2017 I DDC 745.5—dc23
LC record available at https://lccn.loc.gov/2016029712

Printed in the United States of America
Corporate Graphics

ABOUT THE AUTHOR

Dr. Virginia Loh-Hagan is an author, university professor, former classroom teacher, and
curriculum designer. She loves crafts! She created an arts and crafts center at her house.
She lives in San Diego with her very tall husband and very naughty dogs. To learn more
about her, visit www.virginialoh.com.

TABLE OF CONTENTS

CHAPTER ONE

WHAT DOES IT MEAN TO HOST A CRAFT FAIR?

Do you love making art? Do you love making crafts? Do you love selling things? Then, hosting a craft fair is the right project for you!

Craft fairs are organized **retail** events. Retail is selling things for money. People display and trade **wares**. Wares are products or services that are sold. Craft fairs feature **handcrafts**. Handcrafts are things people make with their hands.

People host craft fairs to show off their skills. They host craft fairs to earn money. They need money to support their craft making.

Talk to other people who have hosted craft fairs. Get their opinions.

KNOW THE LINGO

Artisan: a worker in a skilled trade, especially one that involves making things by hand

Artsy-fartsy: pretending to be creative or artistic

Bazaar: marketplace where people sell all kinds of crafts and goods

Flea market: marketplace where people sell secondhand goods

Hobbyist: a person who pursues a specific hobby

Hoopla wall: a wall decorated with art framed in embroidery hoops

Lettering: fancy, decorative letters used for signs

Makerspace: place where people can be creative

Nimble fingers: having quick and agile hands that are able to expertly make crafts

Repurpose: taking trash and giving it another purpose by changing it

Swap meet: event where people trade or sell crafts and/or goods

Vendors: sellers

Host a craft fair whenever you want. They're popular all year long.

Craftsmen have special skills. They create special things. They may use special equipment. They learn their craft. They're trained by other craftsmen. Craft fairs need craftsmen to make products.

Craftsmen also need sales skills. They serve **customers**. Customers buy things.

You'll have fun hosting your own craft fair. You'll make crafts. You'll sell crafts. You'll meet people.

Recruit sellers from other craft fairs. Let them know about your event.

CHAPTER TWO

WHAT DO YOU NEED TO HOST A CRAFT FAIR?

Create a **committee**. This is a group. It's in charge of the craft fair. It takes care of the details.

➡ Assign a **chair**. The chair is the boss.

➡ Assign someone to take care of **publicity**. This person promotes the event.

➡ Assign someone to take care of the **budget**. A budget is a list of costs. This person tracks money. This person ensures there are **profits**. Profit is money earned.

➡ **Assign someone to find sellers. Sellers buy booths. Booths are spaces. This is where people sell their crafts.**

➡ **Assign helpers. They set up. They also clean up.**

Don't spend more than you make.

Decide the type of craft sale you want to host. There are two types. **Juried** craft shows are the first type. They're selective. Juried means a committee judges the crafts.

➡ **Ask sellers to submit applications. Have them include photos and descriptions.**

➡ **Make a list of what you're looking for.**

➡ **Judge the quality of the crafts. Be picky.**

➡ **Accept the crafts you want. Reject the others.**

➡ **Limit the number of each type of crafts.**

Be nice to the sellers you reject. You may want them to participate in future craft shows.

Consider hosting **nonjuried** craft shows. These are not judged.

➡ Allow anyone to sign up. Take as many sellers as you can. Take the first sellers who sign up.

➡ Have them submit applications. This is for your records.

Decide what types of crafts you want to sell.

➡ **Consider wearable crafts. These are things people wear. Examples are jewelry and clothes.**

➡ **Consider homemade foods. Consider baked goods.**

➡ **Consider paper arts. Examples are cards and artwork.**

➡ **Consider pottery. Examples are bowls and vases.**

➡ **Consider toys. Examples are dolls and puppets.**

➡ **Consider recycled items. Some people create art from junk.**

Decide where to host the craft fair.

➡ **Decide to be outdoors or indoors.**

➡ **Choose a place where many people come by. Examples are malls and busy streets.**

➡ **Get permission to be there.**

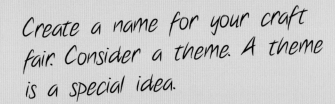

Create a name for your craft fair. Consider a theme. A theme is a special idea.

TRY THIS!

Create a unique display. Stand out. Don't use tables.

You'll need: several wooden crates, three different paints, paintbrushes, picture frames without glass, yarn, clothespins

Steps

1 Empty and clean crates. Paint them in three different colors. Allow to dry.

2 Put your branding on the crates.

3 Stack them on top of each other. Stack them next to each other. Make sure all the crates touch. Create different sizes of rows and columns.

4 Paint picture frames different colors. Allow to dry.

5 Tie yarn to one side of each frame. Wrap yarn around frame several times. First, wrap around the sides. Then, wrap top to bottom. Last, tie to the other side of the frame.

6 Place frames on top of crates. Hook craft items onto yarn. Use clothespins if needed.

7 Display craft items inside crates.

Sell booths to sellers. This is how craft fairs make money.

➡ **Decide fees.**

➡ **Collect money.**

Decide when to host the craft fair.

➡ **Choose a time when people are around.**

➡ **Choose day or night. Day has better light. But night markets are popular, too.**

Get equipment. Include equipment costs in booth fees.

➡ **Get tables and chairs.**

➡ **Get tablecloths.**

➡ **Get power cords. Some sellers may need electricity. Charge them more.**

➡ **Get trash cans.**

Remind sellers to bring their own equipment.

➡ **Have sellers bring signage. Signage is signs. It's about branding. Branding is how a business identifies itself.**

➡ **Have sellers bring shopping bags.**

➡ **Have sellers bring cash boxes or cash aprons. Cash aprons have many pockets. They hold money and change.**

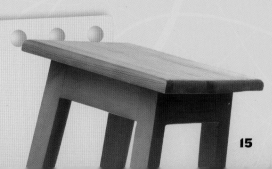

Borrow tables and chairs from friends and family.

CHAPTER THREE

HOW DO YOU SET UP A CRAFT FAIR?

Publicize the craft fair. Make sure people come to the event.

➡ **Make flyers. These are small paper signs. Give details about the events. Post flyers at community centers. Post them at local schools. Give flyers to people.**

➡ **Send several e-mails. Send e-mails right before the event. People need reminders.**

➡ **Share the event on social media.**

➡ **Make big signs. Put these where people can see them.**

Advice from the Field
TOM AND JOE BARRATT

Tom and Joe Barratt are from Great Britain. They're brothers. They founded The Teenage Market when they were teenagers. The Teenage Market is a craft fair for teenagers. It supports people between ages 10 and 29. It gives young people a place to show off their creative skills. It also gives them a chance to learn business skills. The Barratts advise combining retail and live performance. They have trader spaces. They have performer spaces. They also sell snacks and drinks. The Barratts want to support new generations of young traders and performers. They help other towns and cities run their own Teenage Markets. They said, "It's great to see the impact that our events are now making in communities across the country."

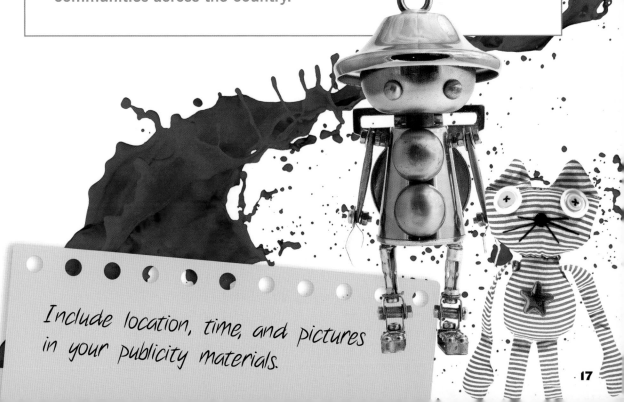

Include location, time, and pictures in your publicity materials.

17

Create a **program**. This is a special book for the event.

➡ **Include all the sellers' information. Include their products and contact information.**

➡ **Upload information to your event's Web site or Facebook page.**

Make sure customers can see prices. They don't like to ask how much things cost.

Give sellers rules about the craft fair. Send them rules before the event.

➡ **Charge extra for things like electricity and extra tables. Decide how much.**

➡ **Decide if sellers can bring extra furniture.**

➡ **Decide if sellers can move around their furniture.**

➡ **Decide how sellers can display their signage.**

Encourage sellers to practice setting up their booths. Have them do **mock displays**. Mock means fake.

➡ **Have sellers create their booths. They arrange things until they're happy.**

➡ **Have sellers take photos of their mock displays. They use the photos to re-create their booths.**

➡ **Have sellers include price tags. The tags should include branding. They should be pretty.**

Be prepared to manage headquarters.

Organize the booths.

➡ **Know your space. Visit the location before the event.**

➡ **Arrange the tables to fit in the space. Arrange them in rows. This is so customers can shop better.**

➡ **Make sure there's plenty of space for tables. Create big aisles. Aisles are walkways. Customers need a lot of room to walk.**

➡ **Make sure booths are big enough. Customers need room to browse.**

➡ **Decide a starting place. Put an information table at the front. This is headquarters. Encourage customers walk through from start to finish. Make sure they can shop at booths on their way.**

➡ **Create a map. Give the map to everyone.**

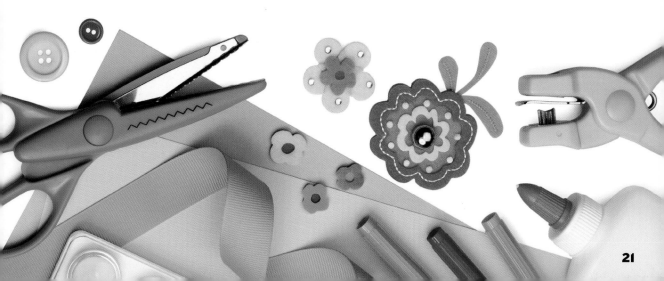

CHAPTER FOUR

HOW DO YOU RUN A CRAFT FAIR?

You're ready for the craft fair! The committee chair makes sure the craft fair is successful.

Do a **walk-through**. Walk-throughs are spot checks. Walk from start to finish. Check the sellers' booths. Make sure everything is visible.

→ Make sure light shines on jewelry.

→ Offer tips on arrangements. Some things need to be dangled. Some need to be on tables.

→ Place crafts where people can see them.

→ Make sure there are no empty spaces. Customers don't like half-empty shelves. They like choices.

Set up headquarters.

➡ **Greet everyone as they come in.**

➡ **Provide a program.**

➡ **Ask customers to sign a mailing list. This is to inform them of future events.**

➡ **Be available to answer questions.**

Replenish sold items with new items.

QUICK TIPS

- Turn your craft fair into a social event. Play music. Host contests.

- Provide a mirror if you are selling wearable goods.

- Don't let your craft items blow away. Bring weights. Clip them to things. Stack items close together.

- Use playing cards to hold necklaces, bracelets, and earrings. Cut slits at the top of the cards. Pull jewelry into the slits to hold in place.

- Bring a friend. You can take turns taking breaks. You can watch for shoplifters.

- Encourage people to look. Don't worry if they don't buy. Having people at your booth attracts customers.

- Be ready when customers praise your work. Don't just say, "Thank you." Instead, say, "Thank you, it's great because . . ."

Create a "crafty tote." This is a special kit to help with emergencies. Things happen. Be prepared. Keep this kit at headquarters.

➡ **Pack pens, paper, and tape.**

➡ **Pack a calculator.**

➡ **Pack a first aid kit.**

➡ **Pack a sewing kit. Include safety pins and scissors.**

➡ **Pack small bills and coins. This is to make change.**

Decide if you want to host your own booth. Feel free to sell your own crafts.

➡ **Make sure someone takes care of your booth. Someone needs to handle money. Someone needs to talk to customers.**

➡ **Put your booth next to headquarters.**

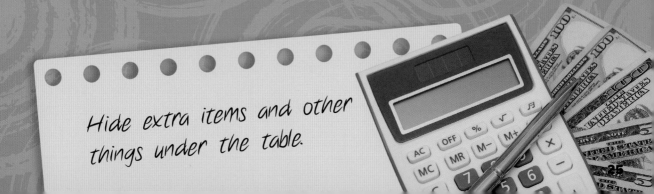

Hide extra items and other things under the table.

Chat with customers. Keep them hanging around to shop more.

Consider selling food. You can make extra money. Customers will hang around. This means they'll stay and shop.

➡ **Sell cold drinks. Examples are water and soda.**

➡ **Sell hot drinks. Examples are tea, coffee, and hot cocoa.**

➡ **Sell snacks. Examples are popcorn and candy.**

➡ **Make sure you aren't competing with sellers. Know the other food items being sold. Don't sell those items.**

Consider hosting craft workshops.

➡ **Teach people how to do a simple craft. Provide the materials. Model the steps.**

➡ **Charge a small fee. Or ask for donations. Donations are money gifts.**

Decide when you will end the craft fair.

➡ **Make an announcement. Give people a warning.**

➡ **Let customers finish shopping before you pack up.**

End the craft fair.

➡ **Pack up. Clean up.**

➡ **Thank the sellers. Make sure they come back to your next event. Give them a special deal for signing up for future events.**

➡ **Review the good and bad. Think about ways to improve.**

➡ **Keep in touch with sellers. Keep in touch with customers. Send a thank-you note. Use the mailing list.**

➡ **Post unsold items online. An example is Etsy. Etsy is an online craft store. People post their crafts to sell to others. Have an adult help you manage your Etsy store.**

Craft fairs continue to grow. Keep working on your craft. Keep sharing your art with the world. And make some money, too!

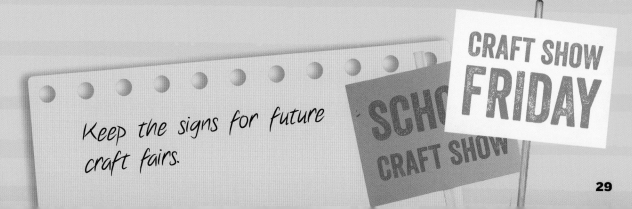

Keep the signs for future craft fairs.

D.I.Y. EXAMPLE!

STEPS	EXAMPLES
Type	Nonjuried Craft Fair ◆ Open to all sellers, any ages ◆ Available to first 30 seller applications
Where	Local high school parking lot, which faces a major street
When	First Saturday of June
My costs	◆ Space rental fee ◆ Business permit fee ◆ Table rental fee (or borrow from family and friends) ◆ Tape (to mark off booth areas) ◆ Programs and promotions ◆ Trash cans and trash bags
Fees	◆ $50 per booth, which includes mention in the program and Web site ◆ $15 per table ◆ $10 for advertisement in program

STEPS	EXAMPLES
Rules	→ Each booth can only have one to two tables. To save money, sellers can bring their own tables as long as they fit in the booth space.
	→ Each booth must keep items inside designated areas. Walkway must be free and clear.
	→ Each booth is responsible for cleaning its own areas.
	→ Sellers must pay fees in advance to secure booth.
Organize craft tables	→ Set up headquarters at the beginning.
	→ Organize two long rows of tables (15 tables in each row).
	→ Group similar products together.
	→ Place food tables at the end.
	→ Place trash cans at several places.

GLOSSARY

aisles (ILEZ) walkways

booths (BOOTHS) spaces for sellers to sell their crafts

branding (BRAND-ing) how a business identifies itself

budget (BUHJ-it) list of costs and profits

cash aprons (KASH AY-pruhnz) aprons with many pockets to hold cash and change

chair (CHAIR) leader of a committee

committee (kuh-MIT-ee) a group of people who plan events

craftsmen (KRAFTS-muhn) people with special skills who are able to make a specific craft

customers (KUHS-tuh-murz) buyers

donations (doh-NAY-shuhnz) gifts of money

flyers (FLYE-urz) papers that promote an event

handcrafts (HAND-krafts) things made by someone's hands

juried (JOOR-eed) a judged event, very selective

mock displays (MAHK dis-PLAYZ) practice displays

nonjuried (nahn-JOOR-eed) an event open to all

profits (PRAH-fits) money earned

program (PROH-gram) special book for the event

publicity (puh-BLIS-ih-tee) promotion

retail (REE-tayl) selling things for money

signage (SINE-ij) signs and banners that help promote

walk-through (WAWK-throo) spot check

wares (WAIRZ) things or services that are sold for money

wearable (WAIR-uh-buhl) crafts that can be worn, such as clothes and jewelry

INDEX

LEARN MORE

BOOKS

Colman, Tina, and Peggie Llanes. *The Hipster Librarian's Guide to Teen Craft Projects*. Chicago: American Library Association, 2008.

Goldschadt, Sarah. *Craft-a-Day: 365 Simple Handmade Projects*. Philadelphia: Quirk Books, 2012.

Martha Stewart's Encyclopedia of Crafts: An A-to-Z Guide with Detailed Instructions and Endless Inspiration. New York: Potter Craft, 2009.

WEB SITES

American Craft Council: http://craftcouncil.org

I Love Craft Booths: https://www.pinterest.com/catshycrafts/i-love-craft-booths/

The Crafts Fair Online: www.craftsfaironline.com